# THE BRITISH MUSEUM

# PERSIAN
## LOVE POETRY

# THE BRITISH MUSEUM
# PERSIAN
# LOVE POETRY

Vesta Sarkhosh Curtis

AND

Sheila R. Canby

THE BRITISH MUSEUM PRESS

*Frontispiece:* Lovers, in the style of 'Abd Allah, Bukhara, *c.* AD 1560–70.
Opaque watercolour on paper (see p.26).

ABBREVIATIONS IN PERSIAN DATES
AH: After Hijra (lunar calendar)
SH: Solar Hijra (solar calendar)
AH 1: AD 622

Photography by British Museum Department of Photography and Imaging
(John Williams and Kevin Lovelock)

First published in 2005 by The British Museum Press
A division of The British Museum Company Ltd
38 Russell Square, London WC1B 3QQ
www.britishmuseum.co.uk
Reprinted 2006, 2007

Vesta Sarkhosh Curtis and Sheila R. Canby have asserted their moral rights
to be identified as the authors of this work

A catalogue record for this book is available from the British Library
ISBN-13: 978-0-7141-2429-2
ISBN-10: 0-7141-2429-X

Designed and typeset in Centaur by Peter Ward
Printed in China by C&C Offset Printing Co., Ltd

# ACKNOWLEDGEMENTS

THIS BOOK would not have been possible without the support and help of a number of people. Above all, Armin Sarkhosh, with his excellent knowledge of Persian literature and love of Persian poetry, made the selection process an unforgettable and enjoyable experience. We are indebted to Paul Luft and Lala Divshali Luft, whose help and suggestions were invaluable, and also to Narguess Farzad. Shahrokh Razmjou typed the Persian texts, while Mehdi and Goli Ahari helped with the Persian software. Parvaneh Sattari sent recent publications from Tehran, and family and friends listened to the Persian love poems and patiently went through various stages of the English translations.

Nina Shandloff of the British Museum Press made a tremendous contribution by sharing the enthusiasm for this project and helping with the editing of the English translations. We also owe special thanks to John Williams and Kevin Lovelock, who have digitally photographed the images. They have been unfailingly helpful, and their skill never disappoints. We are grateful to Dr David Khalili and Nahla Nassar for allowing us to reproduce the image of Ardashir and the slave-girl Gulnar from the *Shahnama* of Shah Tahmasp, and to Massoud Arabshahi and Rose Issa for permission to publish Untitled Red. We would like to thank Venetia Porter for her enthusiastic help with the choice of a contemporary image and Robert Knox for supporting the project.

Finally, this little book must not be regarded as a comprehensive collection of Persian love poetry. It is a small selection which we hope will encourage readers to delve further into the wealth of Persian literature.

The tomb of Hafiz, Shiraz, Iran.

# INTRODUCTION

He who wants to understand the art of poetry
Must go to the land of poetry
He who wants to understand the poet
Must go to the poet's country.

THESE ARE LYRICS of the German poet Goethe (1749–1832) from his *West-Eastern Diwan*, composed between 1813 and 1815. Goethe was much influenced by Persian philosophy and poetry, which had been translated into German and French at the end of the eighteenth century. He expresses his admiration for Persian poets and their love poetry in a number of poems, but he particularly revered Hafiz (d. AH 792/AD 1390).

Foreign visitors to the tombs of the Persian poets Sa'di and Hafiz in the southern Iranian city of Shiraz are often surprised and moved to see how many Iranians, young and old, from all different parts of the country, come to pay homage to two of the most well-known and popular national poets. The same could also be said about the resting places of Firdausi in Tus and Umar Khayyam in Nishabur, both in eastern Iran.

Even after a millennium, people still recite their poetry and easily relate to the lyrics. Poetry is part of the everyday life of almost every Iranian — we are continuously exposed to names such as Rudaki, Firdausi, Umar Khayyam, Sa'di, Hafiz, Maulavi (Rumi), Nizami and many others. It is used to express feelings and thoughts and to seek answers to one's problems. Poetry is much enjoyed by Iranians and other

Persian (Farsi) speakers, who find solace and pleasure not just in the poetic language but also in the poets' philosophical and human approach to life – above all, in a mystic (Sufi) view of the world, reaching truth and God through intense love and devotion. The language of love poetry, as seen in the poems of the three great lyric poets Rumi (d. AH 671/AD 1273), Sa'di (d. *c.* AH 691/AD 1292) and Hafiz as well as many others, is emotional, passionate, highly imaginative, and usually allegoric. It is often impossible to distinguish between mystical and human erotic love. The language is rhythmic like music and, in fact, the mystical poem the Masnavi by Maulavi (Rumi) is often sung in classical Persian music. At the same time, a sense of humour and compassion emerges which enables the modern reader to enjoy the language and relate to the words.

# LANGUAGE

DESPITE THE Arab conquest of Sasanian Iran in the mid seventh century and Islam becoming the new religion, replacing Zoroastrianism, the Indo-European language of Persian was not abandoned in favour of the language of the newcomers. Gradually the Middle Persian language of Sasanian Iran was adapted and transformed into what is called New Persian (Farsi), and its vocabulary incorporated Arabic words. New forms were created for Persian poetry.

A couple of centuries after the Islamic conquest of Iran, local dynasties in Persia actively contributed to the emergence of New Persian and the revival of an older literary tradition. The tenth-century Samanid dynasty, which claimed descent from the pre-Islamic Sasanian kings, was based in Bukhara and Samarkand in Central Asia (modern Uzbekistan). They revived ancient Persian traditions and supported the transformation of vernacular and local dialects into a literary idiom, namely New Persian. It was at the Samanid court that the 'father of Persian poetry', the blind bard Rudaki from Samarkand (d. AH 329/ AD 940), wrote and performed his poems.

Until the nineteenth century, the geographical area in which Persian was spoken covered a much larger region than modern Iran. With the decline of the Ottoman, Safavid and Mughal empires in the eighteenth and nineteenth centuries, the use of Persian proper became confined to the states of Iran, Afghanistan and Tajikistan.

# POETIC FORMS

*Ghazal*: a short poem, *c.* 7–15 lines, all having the same rhyme. The last line normally includes the signature of the poet. Generally resembling the sonnet and used for lyric poetry, it embodies the essence of Persian poetry.

*Masnavi*: based on rhyming couplets and used mainly for longer poems of a narrative or didactic form.

*Qasida*: a long monorhyme, the most favoured form for court poetry, and often used for praising the poet's patron or benefactor.

*Qit'a*: monorhyme, usually 3–20 lines, used for casual subjects, satire, ethical or moralizing themes.

*Ruba'i*: quatrain, best known through Umar Khayyam's amorous and philosophical poems.

*Dau bayti*: a version of the *ruba'i*, mostly occurring in popular poetry.

# HISTORY AND LEGEND

INTEREST IN THE LEGENDS of pre-Islamic Iran did not die out in the centuries following the Arab conquest. It reached a high point in the late tenth and eleventh centuries when, in AD 1010, Firdausi of Tus completed his *Shahnama*. This Book of Kings was based on oral traditions and other ancient histories, in particular the official Sasanian history of the *Khuday-nama*. The original Pahlavi or Middle Persian version was translated into Arabic and then into Persian in the middle of the eighth century. Firdausi's epic in some 55,000 double verses was begun under the patronage of the Samanids but completed during the rule of a new dynasty, the Ghaznavids (AH 367–555/AD 997/8–1160). The *Shahnama* deals in the first part with mythological kings of eastern Iran, who find their equivalent in pre-Islamic Zoroastrian religious literature. The second part of the *Book of Kings* describes the ancient heroes. The most famous of these was Rustam, a supernatural hero, son of Zal and grandson of Sam of the House of Nariman, who defended the borders of the country and saved the king of kings from Afrasiyab, Iran's external enemy. Rustam's devotion to the ruling house was such that he sacrificed everything, even killing his own son Suhrab in battle without realizing who he was. This tragic story was the inspiration for *Sohrab and Rustum* by the nineteenth-century English poet Matthew Arnold.

The third and last part of the *Shahnama* describes Iran's history under Sasanian rule, from Ardashir I (AD 224–41) until the last king Yazdgird III, who succumbed to the forces of the invading Muslim Arabs in AD 652.

Gurgani's eleventh-century *Vis and Ramin* was based on another ancient story, probably of Parthian origin, dating back to the first century AD, which enjoyed popularity in Islamic times. Gurgani (d. AH 442/AD 1050) explains in his opening verses that the original story was in Pahlavi (Middle Persian). The poet must have used a Persian prose version of the love epic and turned it into a romantic poem, claiming he had improved the love story with rhyme and metre. Ramin, a bard and the lover of Vis, a married woman, plays the harp and expresses his passion for her.

A number of other ancient love stories were rewritten in New Persian rhyme. These include tales about the Sasanian king Khusrau II Parviz (AD 590–628) and his Christian wife Shirin, which appear in Firdausi's *Shahnama* as well as in the *Khamsa* (Quintet) of Nizami Ganjavi (d. AH 613/AD 1217).

Jami (d. AH 895/AD 1490), from Khurasan in eastern Iran, followed Nizami in composing several romantic epics, of which the best known is *Yusuf and Zulaikha*. His *Salaman and Absal*, also based on an ancient story, is less familiar, although an English translation of this love story was made in rhyme in 1904 by Edward Fitzgerald, who is better known for his free translations of the Ruba'iyat of Umar Khayyam:

> Now when Salaman's Heart turn'd to Absal
>> Her Star was happy in the Heavens – Old Love
> Put forth afresh – Desire doubled his Bond:
>> And of the running Time she watch'd an Hour
> To creep into the Mansion of her Moon
>> And satiate her soul upon his Lips.
> And the Hour came; she stole into his Chamber –
>> Ran up to him, Life's offer in her Hand –
> And, falling like a Shadow at his Feet,
>> She laid her Face beneath. Salaman then

With all the courtesies of Princely Grace
　　Put forth his Hand – he rais'd her in his Arms –
He held her trembling there – and from that Fount
　　Drew first Desire; then, Deeper from her Lips,
That, yielding, mutually drew from his
　　A Wine that ever drawn from never fail'd –

With the end of the rule of the Il-Khanid Mongols (AH 654–737/ AD 1256–1336) and the Timurids (AH 771–899/AD 1370–1495), and the establishment of the Safavid dynasty (AH 907–1148/AD 1501–1736), Persian poetry moved eastwards to the generous patronage of the court of the Mughal emperors of India.

The nineteenth-century Qajar rulers of Iran showed particular interest in the *Shahnama* and stories about the ancient kings, probably because they were eager to portray themselves as the continuation of an ancient tradition. One of the great poets of this time was Iraj Mirza (1874–1926), a Qajar prince, whose love poetry is often explicitly erotic and daring.

## WOMEN POETS

MODERN PERSIAN POETRY has abandoned the traditional modes and moved to free verse, and there are a number of outstanding Iranian poets. Amongst them are exceptional women such as Parvin Etesami (1906–41), Forugh Farrokhzad (1935–67) and Simin Behbahani (1928–). With many others, they continue a tradition dating back to the ninth century. There is a strong sense of protest and individual engagement in the work of many twentieth-century female poets which echoes the sentiments of several famous medieval voices.

Raba'a Qazdari was a tenth-century woman poet of immense emotion and courage who had a passionate extramarital love affair and ran away with her slave lover, leaving behind her husband and family — for which she was punished with death.

Mahasti Ganjavi, whose real name was Manijeh but who was called by her father 'Mahasti' (you are like a moon) because of her beauty, seems to have enjoyed an important position at the court of the Seljuq ruler Sultan Sanjar (AH 511–52/AD 1118–58). Jahan Malik Khatun, a fourteenth-century contemporary of Hafiz, belonged to an aristocratic family and is best known through her Divan.

T HE THIRTEENTH-CENTURY poet Sa'di called his collection of prose and poetry *Gulistan* (Rose Garden) and his lyrics *Bustan* (Orchard). In his introduction to the *Gulistan*, the poet compares poetry with the paintings of Mani, a third-century prophet and highly competent artist. About his own Gulistan, he says:

> What use is a tray of flowers to you?
>> Take a leaf from my rose garden.
> A rose will only live for five days or six
>> But this rose garden will remain fresh, for ever.

بچه کار آیدت ز گل طبقی      از گلستان من ببر ورقی

گل همین پنج روز و شش باشد    وین گلستان همیشه خوش باشد

Although my heart is full of the sorrow of separation,
  Joy mixed with your sorrow increases my unhappiness.
Every night I think of you and say, oh Lord:
  Here is separation and there is connection.

RUDAKI


شادی بغم توام ز غم افزون است     با آنکه دلم از غم هجرت خونست
هجرانش چنین است وصالش چونست     اندیشه کنم هر شب و گویم یا رب


Kneeling youth with a wine cup, signed by Mu`in Musavvir, Safavid Iran,
Isfahan, dated AH 1[0]74 /AD 1663–4. Opaque watercolour and gold on paper.
By the 1660s, kneeling figures in this pose were almost a standard feature of
Persian painting. This image relies on a series of prototypes dating from the
1580s and early 1600s. As in many other portraits of wine drinkers, the figure
gazes into the distance as if imagining an absent loved one.

At last I was recaptured by his love
  Resisting had no effect
Love is like an ocean without a shore
  How can one swim there, oh wise one?
Love must be taken right to the end
  Many unsuitable things must be accepted
Ugliness must be seen as if it were good
  Poison must be taken as if it were sugar
I was disobedient and did not understand:
  The harder you pull, the tighter the rope.

RABA'A

| | |
|---|---|
| کوشش بسیار نامد سودمند | عشق او باز اندر آوردم به بند |
| کی توان کردن شنا ای هوشمند | عشق دریایی کرانه ناپدید |
| بس که بپسندی باید ناپسند | عشق را خواهی که تا پایان بری |
| زهر باید خورد و انگارید قند | زشت باید دید و انگارید خوب |
| کز کشیدن تنگ تر گردد کمند | توسنی کردم ندانستم همی |

Seated youth reading poetry, signed by Riza-yi ʿAbbasi, Safavid Iran, Isfahan, c. AD 1625. Opaque watercolour, gold and ink on paper. Based on an original portrait by the late-16th-century painter Muhammadi of Herat, this work was produced on the order of Shah ʿAbbas I (r. 1587–1629). The youth's gold brocade cloak signals his courtly status, while his dreamy expression implies that he is contemplating the poetry or an absent lover.

Behind the curtain there was a face like a moon
    Like the shining sun, full of colour and scent.
Rustam spoke to her, asked her name:
    'What are you seeking in the darkness of night? What
    is your desire?'
'Tahmina is my name' was how she replied.
    'Sorrow has cut my heart in two.
Daughter of the king of Samangan am I, and
    From the stock of leopards and panthers.
There is none so royal in the whole world as me –
    Beneath the wheel of the firmament there are very few
    like me.
No man has ever seen me beyond the curtain
    No man has ever heard my voice.'

Rustam and Tahmina, from FIRDAUSI's *Shahnama*

چو خورشید تابان پر از رنگ و بوی     پسش پرده اندر یکی ماهروی

چه جویی شب تار کام تو چیست     بپرسید از او گفت نام تو چیست

تو گویی دل از غم بدو نیمه ام     چنین داد پاسخ که تهمینه ام

Detail of wind-whipped trees against a golden sky, from an unfinished *Shahnama* attributable to Sultan Muhammad, Safavid Iran, Tabriz, *c.* AD 1515–22. Opaque watercolour and ink on paper. Rustam sets out across the dangerous province of Mazandaran to rescue the shah, Kay Kavus. Overcome by fatigue, Rustam lies down in a pasture that turns out to be a lion's lair. As the hero sleeps, the lion returns and attacks Rustam's horse Rakhsh, who ultimately tramples the beast to death.

As soon as I saw you, I died
    I am in turmoil, filled with passion and sorrow.
I cannot see the clear light of day for pain, and so
    The sun has turned to lapis lazuli for me.
Just make me happy in secret
    And return my youth to me.

Sudaba and Siyavush, from FIRDAUSI's *Shahnama*

خروشان و جوشان و آزرده ام   که تا من ترا دیده ام مرده ام

برآنم که خورشید شد لاجورد   همی روز روشن نبینم ز درد

ببخشای روز جوانی مرا   یکی شاد کن در نهانی مرا

A prince and his lady, signed by Ghulamzada Qadimi `Ali (`Ali Quli Jabbihdar),
Safavid Iran, Isfahan, AD 1670–80. Opaque watercolour and gold on paper. A
prince in full regalia, including a turban with a cornucopia of feathers, receives a
flower from a girl, probably a courtesan, in a very low-cut dress and bare feet.
The uncovered face, exposed chest and feet of the woman suggest that she is
physically intimate with the prince, while the glances and poses of the figures
suggest that their relationship has just begun.

When gracefully towards Ardashir she came,
    Clad in jewels and the scent of musk and amber,
She lifted his head from the precious silken pillow
    And, when he awoke, she tightly embraced him.

Gulnar and Ardashir, from FIRDAUSI's *Shahnama*

پر از گوهر و بوی مشک و عبیر     چو آمد خرامان بر اردشیر
چو بیدار شد تنگ در بر گرفت     ز بالین دیبا سرش بر گرفت

Ardashir and the slave-girl Gulnar, from the *Shahnama* of Shah Tahmasp, attributed to Mir Musavvir, Safavid Iran, Tabriz, dated AH 934/AD 1527–8. Opaque watercolour, gold and ink on paper. Having spied the handsome Sasanian Prince Ardashir at the Parthian court, the slave-girl Gulnar slides down a rope into his pavilion in the middle of the night. He awakens and, amazed by her beauty, welcomes her into his bed.

In every way I tried to show you,
>   But not once were you moved by fatherly feelings.
Now open my cuirass
>   And look at my fair naked body . . .
The thought of my departure made my mother exhausted
>   An amulet around my arm she tied
And told me it had once been yours:
>   Take it and see when it can be of any use.
When Rustam opened the cuirass and saw the amulet
>   He tore all his clothes,
Lamented and pulled his hair, and
>   Threw earth on his head, tears flowing down his face.

The fatal battle between Rustam and Suhrab,
from FIRDAUSI's *Shahnama*

چو بگشاد خفتان و آن مهره دید   همه جامه بر سر خویشتن بر درید
همی ناله کرد و همی کند موی   سری پر ز خاک و پر از آبروی

Rustam beside his dying son Suhrab, signed by Mu`in Musavvir, Safavid
Iran, Isfahan, dated AH 1059/AD 1649. Opaque watercolour and ink on paper.
Suhrab, Rustam's son who has never seen his father, leads an army against Iran.
Unaware that he is fighting his own son, Rustam stabs Suhrab. Upon removing
Suhrab's armour, Rustam discovers to his horror the amulet he had given to
Suhrab's mother.

I wanted two kisses from her ruby lips and begged:
    Raise this mean creature with this kiss.
She said: One is enough – if you get two
    You will rebel. This I know from much experience.
My kiss is a second life – never has
    Anyone received another life.

FARRUKHI SISTANI

خواستم از لعل او دو بوسه و گفتم      تربیتی کن بآب لطف خسی را

گفت یکی بس بود وگر دو ستانی      فتنه شوی آزموده ایم بسی را

عمر دوباره است بوسه من و هرگز      عمر دوباره نداده اند کسی را

Lovers, in the style of `Abd Allah, modern Uzbekistan, Bukhara, c. AD 1560–70.
Opaque watercolour on paper. Paintings such as this often accompanied poetry
but did not actually illustrate specific narrative passages. Here the woman, with
her hennaed hands, holds a fruit beyond her lover's grasp, perhaps symbolizing
the unattainability of her love.

And then Vis made an oath
  Never to break her alliance with him.
To Ramin she gave a bunch of violets:
  Remember me by this, she said, for ever
Wherever you see such fresh violets in abundance
  Remember this oath and pact.
Thus they both took an oath
  In love and friendship they sealed a pact.
Then the two slept together
  And spoke about the past.

GURGANI, *Vis and Ramin*

که هرگز نشکند با دوست پیوند پس آنگه ویس با وی خورد سوگند

به یادم دار گفتا این همیشه به رامین داد یک دسته بنفشه

ازین پیمان و این سوگند یاد آر کجا بینی بنفشه تازه بر بار

به مهر و دوستی پیمان بکردند چو زین سان هردوان سوگند خوردند

Woman holding two bouquets, from an album of Persian costumes, Qajar Iran, dated AD 1842. Opaque watercolour on paper. While this woman's veil and high-necked dress establish her respectability, the two posies she holds may indicate that she has gathered the flowers for her beloved.

Around Vis Ramin put his arm
> Like a golden necklace around a tall fair cypress.

If they were seen from Paradise
> No one would have been more beautiful

The bed full of flowers and precious stones
> The pillows full of musk and amber

Lips upon lips, and face turned to face
> Playful like a ball in a field

The closeness, holding the beloved,
> Turned their two bodies into one —

If rain had fallen on these two fair bodies
> A raindrop would not have moistened their chests.

GURGANI, *Vis and Ramin*

چو زرین طوق گرد سرو سیمین      در آورده به ویسه دست رامین

ندانستی که نیکوتر ازیشان      گر ایشان را بدیدی چشم رضوان

همه بالین پر از مشک و ز عنبر      همه بستر پر از گل بود و گوهر

در افگنده به میدان از خوشی گوی      لب اندر لب نهاده روی بر روی

Belt buckle, Parthian Iran, 1st–3rd century AD. Leaded copper alloy.
This buckle has been cast in the form of an embracing couple, with a bearded
man on the left and his beloved on the right. Belts were important parts of the
royal insignia in ancient times and were often presented by the 'king of kings'
to his loyal subjects. Elaborate buckles and plaques decorated the belts of kings,
their entourage and high officials in the Parthian and Sasanian periods.

Because of what I see and feel, I scream —
What the eye sees, the heart remembers.
I will forge a dagger with a tip of steel and
Destroy my sight to set free my heart.

BABA TAHIR URYAN

ز دست دیده و دل هر دو فریاد     هر آنچه دیده بیند دل کند یاد
بسازم خنجری نیشش ز فولاد     زنم بر دیده تا دل گردد آزاد

Untitled Red, by Massoud Arabshahi (b. 1935), Tehran, Iran, dated 1981.
Mixed media on paper, Avesta Monotype series. The artist is associated with
the Saqqakhaneh, the most influential contemporary art movement in Iran after
the Second World War, which aimed to combine aspects of Iranian religious folk
art with modernism. The imagery of magical symbols in this work is typical
of their style.

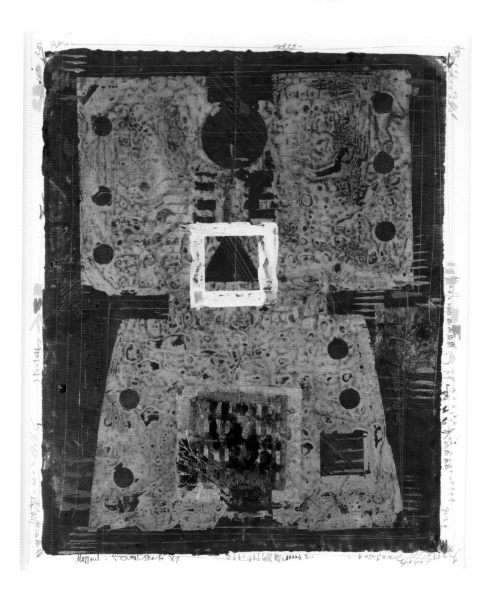

This jug, like me, was once a weeping lover
     Like me, entangled in the locks of a beauty, imprisoned.
This handle that you see around its neck
     Is the hand which once was around the neck of a beloved.

KHAYYAM

در بند سر زلف نگاری بودست      این کوزه چو من عاشق زاری بودست

دستی است که بر گردن یاری بودست      این دسته که بر گردن او می بینی

Bird on a branch, signed by Mirza Aqa-yi Isfahani, Qajar Iran, dated
AH 1243/AD 1827–8. Opaque watercolour on paper. Whereas the foliage and
fruit in this picture lack the brilliant colours of the artist's rosebushes, the bird
with its red back, yellow breast and blue head catches the viewer's attention.
From the 17th century onwards, probably in response to European prototypes,
bees and other insects were included in Persian bird and flower paintings.

رقم کمترین میرزا آقای اصفهانی
۱۳۴۲

Give me three kisses, oh moon-faced beloved, I said.

    She replied, Who in this world has been kissed by the moon?

The radiance of your face increases in the night, I said.

    She replied, It is the moon that lights up the night sky.

I have never seen you stay motionless in one place, I said.

    She replied, It is the eclipse of the moon that bewildered mankind.

MU'IZZI NISHABURI

گفتا که ماه بوسه کرا داد در جهان     گفتم مرا سه بوسه ده ای ماه دلستان

گفتا بشب فروغ دهد ماه آسمان     گفتم فروغ روی تو افزون بود بشب

گفت از خسوف ماه بود خلق را فغان     گفتم بیک مکانت نبینم بیک قرار

A woman tambourinist, from an album of Persian costumes, Qajar Iran, dated AD 1842. Opaque watercolour on paper. Kneeling on a small carpet, this woman holds up a large tambourine called a *daf*, which is played by both men and women, often in combination with other instruments and singers.

Last night, from the palm of the love-selling beauty,
I drank the wine of union until the morning.
Tonight, with a hundred thousand screams and cries,
I wait — when will there be another night like that?

ANVARI

دوش از کف دست آن بت عشق فروش    تا روزِ میِ وصال می کردم نوش
امشب من و صد هزار فریاد و خروش    تا باز شبی کیم بود چون شب دوش

A lady holding a cup, Safavid Iran, Isfahan, early 17th century AD. Opaque
watercolour on paper. This elaborately clad lady offers a tiny cup of wine to
an unseen recipient. The painting, intended for inclusion in an album, may have
been placed on a page facing either a similar composition or a picture of a
young man looking in the direction of this young lady.

Heaven has no other prayer niche but love
Without love the world is worthless.
Become the slave to love, this is the course
This is the path for all pious people.

Introduction to *Khusrau and Shirin*
by NIZAMI GANJAVI

جهان بر خاک عشق آبی ندارد     فلک جز عشق محرابی ندارد
همه صاحبدلانرا پیشه این است   غلام عشق شو کاندیشه این است

Picnic in the countryside, Safavid Iran, Isfahan, *c.* AD 1640. Ink, watercolour
and gold on paper. This gathering has all the components of a romantic Persian
get-together. Alongside food, wine and fainting youths, a dervish observes
pensively from the left and a musician plucks the strings of a lute (`ud) inside
an arched chamber, perhaps a tomb.

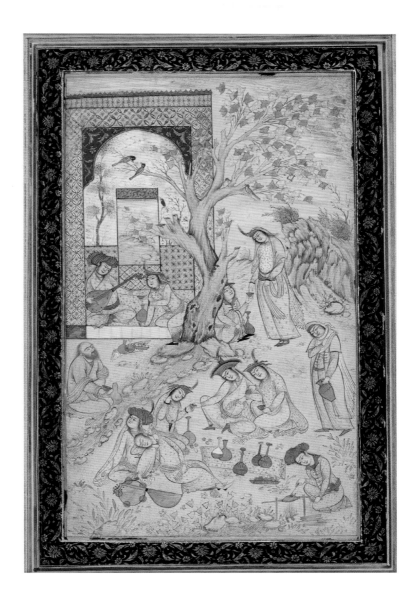

Love came and ransacked the house
    And raised the sword of recklessness
It gave them sorrow and stole their hearts
    Giving their hearts to each other
They lost their tranquillity.
    They fell prey to gossip
Their cover was torn in every way
    Their secret heard in every alleyway.

From *Laili and Majnun* by NIZAMI GANJAVI

برداشته تیغ لاابالی     عشق آمد و کرد خانه خالی

وز دل شدگی قرارشان برد     غم داد دل از کنارشان برد

در معرض گفتگو فتادند     زان دل که به یکدگر نهادند

این پرده دریده شد ز هر سوی   وان راز شنیده شد بهر کوی

Bird and flowers, Qajar Iran, mid 19th century. Opaque watercolour on paper. Birds perched amongst ebullient blossoms were extremely popular in 18th- and 19th-century Iran and are analogous to the poetic motif of *gul o bulbul* (rose and nightingale). Botanical accuracy was not a major concern, as the combination of roses and hydrangea in one plant demonstrates, though these flowers and the primula at lower right are recognizable as species.

When Majnun arrived at the tent
    Drunkenly he began to sing
Speaking the name of Laili and being stoned
    He danced merrily as the stones rained on him.

From *Laili and Majnun* by Nizami Ganjavi

چون بر در خیمه ای رسیدی    مستانه سرود بر کشیدی

لیلی گفتی و سنگ خوری    در خوردن سنگ رقص کردی

Majnun before the tent of Laili, from a *Khamsa* of Nizami, Timurid Iran, *c.* AD 1430. Opaque watercolour and ink on paper. In the story of Laili and Majnun, a young Arab boy named Qais is driven mad by his unrequited love for Laili, daughter of the head of a rival clan. As a result he goes to live in the desert and comes to be called Majnun, which means 'crazy one'. Here an old crone, one of the stock figures in Persian painting, brings Majnun in chains to the tent of his beloved Laili.

Each night, with sorrow for you, a new hardship I see
In my sight, instead of sleep, tears I see
When, like your narcissus, I go to sleep,
A dream I have, more dishevelled than your hair.

MAHASTI GANJAVI

در دیده بجای خواب آبی بینم      هر شب ز غمت تازه عذابی بینم

آشفته تر از زلف تو خوابی بینم      وانگه که چو نرگس تو خوابم ببرد

A lady watching her dog drink from a bowl, signed by Mir Afzal Tuni,
Safavid Iran, Isfahan, *c.* AD 1640. Opaque watercolour, gold and ink on paper.
The figure's pose, her rolled-up dress revealing her belly and flowered underwear,
and the inclusion of a small dog all contribute to the erotic tone of this painting.
Her appearance is consistent with many descriptions by European travellers of
Persian courtesans, who were officially tolerated in part because they paid
substantial taxes.

Listen to the reed flute and its tale,
   Complaining of separation:
Since they cut me off from the bed of reeds
   Men and women lament the sound of my cry.
Due to separation, I want chests torn to shreds
   To describe the pain of desire
Anyone distant from his origins
   Will seek to return to them.
Lamenting at every gathering,
   I am the friend of both the happy and the unhappy
Each believes himself to be my friend,
   Yet none searches for my secrets.
My secret is not far from my lamentation,
   Yet my eyes and ears do not have that light.

*The Tale of the Reed Flute* by MAULANA JALAL AL-DIN BALKHI,
known as RUMI

بشنو از نی چون حکایت می کند     از جدایی ها شکایت می کند

کز نیستان تا مرا ببریده اند     از نفیرم مرد و زن نالیده اند

Clump of violets, from an album of flower drawings, with the seal of Shafi`
`Abbasi, Safavid Iran, Isfahan, dated AH 5 Muharram 1054/14 March 1644. Ink
and watercolour on paper. This delicate drawing of violets may have been
inspired by a European herbal, as are many of the images in the same album.
The artist Shafi` `Abbasi worked at the court of Shah `Abbas II, where he
specialized in bird and flower paintings and drawings.

Come, I am lovesick and desolate without you
　　Come and see how sick I am in this sorrow without you
At night I lament your absence, oh fairy-faced,
　　And when the morning comes, it is as if I am on fire without you.

Sa'di

بیا که در غم عشقت مشوشم بی تو　　بیا ببین که در این غم چه ناخوشم بی تو
شب از فراق تو مینالم ای پری رخسار　چو روز گردد گویی در آتشم بی تو

Yusuf before Zulaikha, from a *Haft Aurang* of Jami, Safavid Iran, Khurasan,
AD 1560–70. Opaque watercolour, gold and ink on paper. When Yusuf enters
the presence of Zulaikha and the women of Egypt, who are paring fruit, they
are so overcome by his beauty that they cut their fingers and swoon. Yusuf is
customarily depicted with a flaming aureole.

I am the servant of the one who steals a heart,
 Or falls in love with the one who gives life.
He who is neither lover nor beloved
 May not even be found in the realm of God.


SA'DI


من چاکر آنم که دلی برباید    یا دل به کسی دهد که جان آساید

آنکس که نه عاشق و معشوق کسیست   در ملک خدای اگر نباشد شاید


A prince entertained in the countryside, attributable to Muhammad Qasim,
seal of Shah `Abbas II, Safavid Iran, Isfahan, *c.* AD 1650. Opaque watercolour, ink
and gold on paper. By torchlight a young prince leaning against a tree is served
wine and entertained by three female musicians. Such soirées were the setting for
flirtations, often made manifest through the recitation of poetry.

Though I am old, hold me tight in your arms at night
So at dawn I will rise beside you as a young man.

HAFIZ

گرچه پیرم تو شبی تنگ در آغوشم کش    تا سحرگه ز کنار تو جوان برخیزم

A kneeling man with a book of poetry, signed by Muhammad Qasim, Safavid
Iran, Isfahan, *c.* AD 1650. Ink and watercolour on paper. This figure holds a *safina*
(oblong-shaped book of poetry) and gazes up towards the sky as if pondering or
perhaps memorizing what he has been reading. Such books were a perfect format
for *ghazals* (short love poems).

At the beginning, your beauty shone with rays of glory
Love came and set the whole world on fire.

Hafiz

در ازل پرتو حسنت ز تجلی دم زد     عشق پیدا شد و آتش به همه عالم زد

Flowers and bees, from an album of flower drawings signed by Shafi` `Abbasi,
Safavid Iran, Isfahan, dated AH Muharram 1050/April 1640. Ink on paper.
Although an inscription identifies these flowers as hyacinths, they more closely
resemble bluebells. The inscription that includes the signature states that the
drawing was completed in the *madrasa* of Maulana Abdullah, which is at the
northern end of the Maidan, the large central square, in Isfahan.

I said I felt pain for you; you said my pain would pass.
  I asked you to be my moon; you said, if she appears.
I said, learn from lovers the custom of faithfulness;
  You said seldom is this the custom of the moon-faced.
I said I wanted to hold your attention;
  You said it is like a night thief and will come another way.

HAFIZ

گفتم که ماه من شو گفتا اگر برآید    گفتم غم تو دارم گفتا غمت سرآید

گفتا ز ماه رویان این کار کمتر آید    گفتم ز مهرورزان رسم وفا بیاموز

گفتا که شبرو است او از راه دیگر آید    گفتم که بر خیالت راه نظر ببندم

Seated dervish, Safavid Iran, Isfahan, *c.* AD 1640. Ink on paper. This figure
can be identified as a dervish by his long sleeves, which extend over his hands.
Although it is not certain what he is contemplating, he gazes up towards the sky
and appears to be detached mentally from his surroundings, possibly meditating
on spiritual matters.

The lover left, not noticing my sad heart
    And shunned my worldly burning sigh
My tears covered the earth, from one end to another
    The unfaithful lover did not even pass my way
My sigh left me and reached seventh heaven
    And had no effect whatsoever on his hard heart.

JAHAN MALIK KHATUN

وز آه سوزناک جهانی حذر نکرد      دلبر برفت و بر دل تنگم نظر نکرد

بگرفت اشک ما دو جهان سربسر ولی   آن بی وفا ز لطف سوی ما گذر نکرد

آهم گذشت و بر فلک هفتمین رسید      وز هیچ نوع در دل سختش اثر نکرد

Kneeling woman counting on her fingers, signed by Mu`in Musavvir,
Safavid Iran, Isfahan, dated Wednesday the 3rd day of Ramadan AH 1[0]84/
12 December 1674. Opaque watercolour, gold and ink on paper. Although
this painting appears to be a portrait, its composition is based on a painting
of the 1620s by Riza, the artist's teacher, which portrayed the wife of a
Safavid government official. The sitter's abstracted expression may reflect her
concentration on counting, or her mind may be wandering elsewhere.

I had vowed never to give my heart to anyone again.
　　But what should I do? Once more I am caught in a passion.
My sigh at dawn will stop the morning breeze
　　When one night I let out a sigh at the top of your lane.

KHAJU KIRMANI

چکنم باز گرفتار شدم در هوسی　　در دلم بود کزین پس ندهم دل بکسی

گر شبی بر سر کوی تو بر آرم نفسی　　نفس صبح فرو بندد از آه سحرم

The carpenter of Sarandib, his unfaithful wife and her lover, from a *Kalila wa Dimna* of Nasr Allah, Inju Iran, Shiraz, AD 1333. Opaque watercolour and ink on paper. The unfaithful wife, seen here in bed with her lover, avoids severe punishment for her infidelity because she notices her husband's foot poking out from under the bed and quickly contrives a story to convince him of her innocence.

Today, separated from my love, I am
    Without companion, sweetheart and friend, I am
The one who did not sleep in the darkness of night, I am
    In short, entangled in every sorrow, I am.

NASIBI GILANI

امروز جدا مانده ز دلدار منم    بی مونس و بی رفیق و بی یار منم
آنکس که نخفت در شب تار منم    القصه بهر غمی گرفتار منم

Youth with cup and bottle, signed by Mir Yusuf, Safavid Iran, Isfahan, *c.* AD 1645.
Opaque watercolour and gold on paper. This figure can be identified as a
European by his hat and cape, although the gold brocade of his trousers would
certainly have been of Iranian manufacture. The face of a woman or beardless
youth on the bottle he holds may be that of the sitter's beloved, in which case
this painting would be a clever double portrait. The artist, also known as
Muhammad Yusuf, was active during the reign of Shah `Abbas II (r. 1642–66).

If you wish, I shall put my fingers together
    And form a stirrup with my two palms
So you can put your foot in my hands
    And warm yourself in my heart
Or put the soles of your feet on my shoulders
    And slip down into my arms.
Softly and lightly, let me embrace you
    So I can spread you like grass on the ground.

IRAJ MIRZA

خواهی اگر پنجه به هم افکنم      وز دو کف دست رکابی کنم

تا تو نهی بر کف من پای خود      گرم کنی در دل من جای خود

یا که بنه پا به سر دوش من      سُر بخور از دوش در آغوش من

نرم و سبکروح بیا در برم      تات چو سبزه به زمین گسترم

Bahram Gur hunts while Fitna plays the harp, from a *Khamsa* of Nizami, signed by Nadim, Mughal India, *c.* AD 1610. Opaque watercolour and ink on paper. Egged on by his slave-girl Fitna, the renowned hunter-king Bahram Gur shoots two arrows into the head of a doe so that it resembles a buck with two 'antlers'. Meanwhile, Fitna strums her harp.

67

Love came, and away went patience and fortitude,
    As did endurance and tranquillity, comfort and sleep.
This flame of love set my heart on fire
    This flood of love drowned me.

SARKHOSH

عشق آمد و رفت طاقت و تاب      هم صبر و سکون و راحت و خواب
زین شعله بجان فتاد آتش      زین سیل گذشت از سرم آب

Youth drinking from a golden cup, Safavid Iran, Isfahan, mid 17th century AD.
Ink, watercolour and gold on paper. Such images suggest a lovelorn youth
yearning for his absent beloved, but drinking wine was also seen as a means of
achieving oneness with God.

The sky like the surface of my heart,
    Is lit by the light of the full moon.
Tonight I escape from sweet sleep
    For the thought of you is much sweeter than sleep.
Staring at the wild shadows of the willow,
    I crawl into the solitude of my bed,
Once again seeking a favourite melody,
    I rest my head on my manuscript.
The bodies of hundreds of tunes dance
    In the dainty crystal of my song.
An unknown pleasure, the colour of dreams,
    Runs like blood through my veins;
On my lips the flames of your kiss
    Blossom like tulips in need of desire
In my thoughts a star full of light
    Shines in a crescent of secrets;
Unaware of the world of dreams
    Venus throws to me a glance of love.
On my manuscript I write the words:
    Be eternal, oh dawn of love.

FORUGH FARROKHZAD

آسمان چون صفحه دل من
روشن از جلوه های مهتاب است
امشب از خواب خوش گریزانم
که خیال تو خوشتر از خواب است

Portrait of Mani the painter, Safavid Iran, Isfahan, *c.* AD 1610, inscribed 'portrait of Mani the painter, beggar[?] of the word'. Opaque watercolour, gold and ink on paper. The inscription refers to the legendary pre-Islamic painter and religious figure Mani, whose name was invoked as an example of artistic excellence, and the portrait provides useful information about the working methods of Safavid painters. Seated with one knee bent up to steady the page, the artist dips the pen in a small ceramic bottle of ink and gazes into the distance above his pince-nez spectacles before embarking on his work.

Why do you ask me the colour of his eyes?
  When did the colour of his eyes ever capture me?
The fire that sparked from his eyes
  Was what ensnared this mad heart.

Forugh Farrokhzad

رنگ چشمش را چه میپرسی زمن
رنگ چشمش کی مرا پابند کرد
آتشی کز دیدگانش سرکشید
این دل دیوانه را دربند کرد

Young dervish, Safavid Iran, Isfahan, *c.* AD 1630. Opaque watercolour on paper. Young men who joined dervish communities served as spiritual apprentices to the older dervishes of their lodge. Often these figures are portrayed with burn marks on their arms, symbolizing the power of love for God in overcoming physical pain or weakness.

73

Without you, away from the beatings of your heart
　　There, my heart rots away under the soil.
Later, wind and rain will wash away softly
　　My name from the face of the stone.
My grave will remain unknown along the path
　　With no tales of name and shame.

FORUGH FARROKHZAD

بی تو دور از ضربه های قلب تو
قلب من می پوسد آنجا زیر خاک
بعد ها نام مرا باران و باد
نرم می شویند از رخسار سنگ
گور من گمنام می ماند براه
فارغ از افسانه های نام و ننگ

Dervish blowing a horn, Safavid Iran, Isfahan, AD 1620s. Opaque watercolour and gold on paper. The mystical form of Islam practised by dervishes is concerned with the individual's quest for union with God. In poetry, the longing for an absent lover often serves as a metaphor for this metaphysical search. The horn, begging-bowl and animal-skin cloak are typical attributes of dervishes, particularly those of the Naqshbandi order.

No, she has not yet died, because I am still alive
    She is alive in my sorrow, my poem and my fantasy
Whatever poetic heritage I have is hers
    Can the centre of love and beauty be ever silenced
And that sweet woman die – she, who bore Shahriyar?
    'Never will die the one whose heart is alive with love'.

SHAHRIYAR

نه او نمرده است که من زنده ام هنوز

او زنده است در غم و شعر و خیال من

میراث شاعرانه من هرچه هست ازوست

کانون مهر و ماه مگر می شود خموش؟

آن شیرین زن بمیرد؟ او شهریار زاد!

هرگز نمیرد آنکه دلش زنده شد بعشق

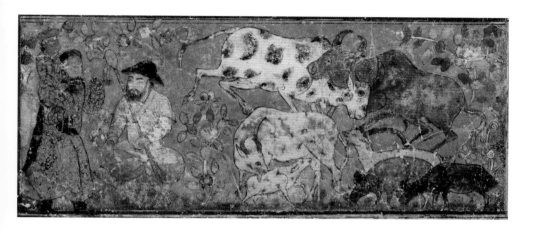

Faridun is given by his mother into the safekeeping of the cowherd, from
the 'Second Small *Shahnama*', Il-Khanid Iran, early 14th century AD. Opaque
watercolour, gold and ink on paper. The child Faridun is depicted at left on the
shoulder of his mother. The evil king Zahhak dreams that Faridun will defeat
him, so the boy is entrusted to the care of the cowherd who owns Pirmaya,
a marvellous cow who becomes Faridun's foster mother.

Without you at a night of full moon, once again I walked through
  that lane
  I was all eyes, bedazzled I searched for you.
The joy of seeing you overflowed the jug of my existence
  I became the same mad lover I was before.

FEREYDOUN MOSHIRI

بی‌تو مهتاب شبی باز از آن کوچه گذشتم
همه تن چشم شدم خیره به دنبال تو گشتم
شوق دیدار تو لبریز شد از جام و جودم
شدم آن عاشق دیوانه که بودم

Young man holding a cup and pomegranate, Safavid Iran, Qazvin, c. AD 1595.
Opaque watercolour and gold on paper. Having removed his voluminous
turban, this young man rests on a rock, daydreaming. The gold wine cup in his
right hand and the pomegranate in his left are the standard accoutrements of
such reveries, suggesting thoughts — sometimes happy, sometimes sad — of an
absent lover.

I said there would always be a bench
Under a tree
In the mystic solitude of a garden.
And I did not say that without you the garden would die
And in the sunny shroud of the beach
The scent of oranges and palm trees would fade.
I said I would throw the stars at your feet.
I did not say that without you, one must doubt the sun
And without you every star is blind.
Come with me
And let us rush towards our shadows
Who are in love.

LAILA KASRA AFSHAR

گفتم همیشه نیمکتی است
زیر یک درخت
و در سکوت عارفانه یک باغ
و نگفتم که بی تو باغ می میرد

*Rabab* player, from an album of Persian and Indian paintings and calligraphy, signed by Muhammad Ja`far, Safavid Iran, Qazvin, *c.* AD 1590. Opaque watercolour and gold on paper. A young dandy rests on a rock to pluck a tune on his *rabab*. The flowers, butterfly and now-blackened pool of the setting suggest that it is springtime, while the figure's sword, quiver and loosened collar may identify him as a reluctant soldier who would rather play love-songs than make war.

Like a tree in spring, my life is full of blossom,
      I have a lap full of flowers – who should I give them to?
Oh, breeze of life, come to me tonight,
      As otherwise, I will not last so full of flowers until dawn.

SIMIN BEHBEHANI

چون درخت فروردین پر شکوفه شد جانم      دامنی ز گل دارم، بر چه کس بیفشانم
ای نسیم جان پرور، امشب از برم بگذر      ورنه این چنین پُر گل تا سحر نمی مانم

Bird, bees and roses, signed by Mirza Aqa-yi Isfahani, Qajar Iran, AH 1243/
AD 1827–8. Opaque watercolour and gold on paper. Qajar painters of bird and
flower pictures sometimes depicted rosebushes growing out of the soil and
sometimes (as here) as separate branches.

Like a flower I shall embrace your love
    And then switch off the light of reason.
I shall place my head between your breasts,
    I drink love from the scent of your body.

HOMA KATOUZIAN

من عشق ترا چو گل در آغوش کنم
وانگاه چراغِ عقل خاموش کنم
سر را به میان سینه ات بگذارم
از عطر تن تو عشق را نوش کنم

Bird in a rosebush, from a Qajar album dated 22 Shawwal AH 1252/30 January
1837. Opaque watercolour on paper. The rose and the nightingale was a popular
poetic and artistic image in 18th- and 19th-century Iran. The motif appears not
only in works on paper, but also on laquerware and textiles.

Everyone's heart is broken one way or another
Whether by strangers or by friends
There is no objection if it is broken by a stranger,
But by the friend, why?

NAHID YOUSEFI

هرکس بطریقی دل را می شکند     بیگانه جدا، دوست جدا می شکند
بیگانه اگر می شکند، حرفی نیست   از دوست بپرسید، چرا می شکند؟!

The fate of the fickle old man, from a *Haft Aurang* of Jami, signed by
Mu`in Musavvir, false signature of Riza-yi `Abbasi, Safavid Iran, Isfahan, dated
AH 1057/AD 1647–8. Opaque watercolour and gold on paper. An old hunchback
declares his love for a beautiful youth while they stand together on a rooftop.
The youth points to a more handsome young man behind him and, when the
old man turns to look, the youth pushes him off the roof. The moral is that
it is impossible to have more than one true love.

Like the essence of a song, I understand you
    I understood your language right from the beginning
Someone writes your words in your eyes
    I understand as soon as your glance flies towards me.
I read you in every verse of the book of emotions
    I feel you, I understand you more than I can express.

Nahid Yousefi

زبانت را نه از امروز، از آغاز می فهمم      تو را اندازه گل بیت یک آواز می فهمم

نگاهت تا بسویم می کند پرواز، می فهمم      کسی در چشمهایت می نویسد حرف هایت را

تو را حس می کنم بالاتر از ابراز می فهمم      ترا در بیت بیت دفتر احساس می خوانم

Woman playing the *santur* (zither), from an album of Persian costumes, Qajar Iran, dated AD 1842. Opaque watercolour on paper. European travellers to Iran in the 19th century collected pictures of local people engaged in typical pursuits and occupations. The *santur*, an instrument of great antiquity, is played by striking the strings with wooden hammers called *mezrab*s. It was introduced to Europe from the Middle East by the Crusaders.

I am a woman
Who has not buried love alive in her body
The desert that screams: Rain on me.
My heart is heavy
I am a woman
Banished from the abode of the gods.
Let the green-tongued ones of unknown love
Reproach Raba'a and Forugh.
Women who
Love the raw passion of love
Women who, with their pains, cannot be confined
Women who do not hide
Their feelings in the corners of their scarves or behind their veils
Or under the carpet.

Parvin Jahanbani


من یک زنم
که عشق را در جانش زنده بگور نکرد
کویری که فریاد زد: بر من ببار
من دلم گرفته است

The Queen of Sheba and the hoopoe, Safavid Iran, Qazvin, *c.* AD 1590. Opaque watercolour and ink on paper. Bilqis, the Queen of Sheba, reclines beside a meandering stream while holding a love letter which the hoopoe, perched in a bush at her feet, will deliver to her beloved, King Solomon. The remarkable arabesque design on Bilqis's dress, incorporating human heads and birds, may allude to the separation of lovers and the role of the hoopoe as their go-between.

# BIOGRAPHICAL NOTES

ANVARI, Uhud al-Din Muhammad, from Abivard, near Sarakhs in Khurasan in eastern Iran. He was originally known as 'Khavari' because of his association with Abivard in Dasht-i Khavaran. After studying astrology, he became a poet at the court of the Seljuq ruler, Sultan Sanjar (AH 511–52/AD 1118–58). He lived in Marv, Balkh and then Nishabur, and also visited Baghdad and Mosul. Anvari died in Balkh (modern Afghanistan) *c.* AH 565/AD 1169–70.

BABA TAHIR URYAN, born *c.* AH 390/AD 1000 in western Iran, either in Luristan or Hamadan, also wrote poetry in dialect. He died in Hamadan after AH 447/AD 1055.

BEHBEHANI, Simin, born 1928 in Tehran. She has published a series of poetical works, including *Sitar-i shikasta* (The broken lute) in 1951, *Jay-i pa* (Footprint) in 1954, *Dasht-i Arzhan* (The Arzhan plain) in 1983 and *Yik daricha-yi azadi* (A window of freedom) in 1995.

FARROKHZAD, Forugh, born AD 1935 in Tehran. She married at sixteen and separated from her husband in 1954. In 1955 her first collection of forty-four poems, *Asir* (Captive), appeared. In 1956 she spent nine months in Europe and in 1964 her fourth poetry collection comprising thirty-five poems, *Tavallodi digar* (Another birth), was published. She died in a car accident 14 February 1967.

FARRUKHI Sistani, Abu'l Hasan, from Sistan in southeastern Iran, poet of the Ghaznavid period. He died AH 429/AD 1037–8.

FIRDAUSI, Hakim Abu'l Qasim, from Tus in Khurasan in eastern Iran. The compilation of the *Shahnama* (The Book of Kings) is based on the pre-Islamic Sasanian *Khuday-nama*, other official histories and an oral tradition. It consists of *c.* 55,000 double verses and was completed in AD 1010. Firdausi died *c.* AH 411/AD 1020.

GURGANI, Farrukh al-Din As'ad. His *Vis and Ramin*, which is often compared with *Tristan and Isolde*, was composed between AD 1040 and 1054. It is based on a pre-Islamic story from the Parthian period in the first century AD.

HAFIZ Shirazi, Khaja Shams al-Din Muhammad, born *c.* AH 726/AD 1325–6 in Shiraz. He was briefly in Isfahan and Yazd but spent most of his life in Shiraz. He died AH 792/AD 1390. His *ghazals* were translated into English by Gertrude Bell and A. J. Arberry.

IRAJ MIRZA, Jalal al-Mamalik, born AH 1291/AD 1874 into the Qajar aristocracy. At nineteen he became the court poet of Muzaffarud-Din Shah, but soon gave up this position and moved to Tabriz, where he took up an administrative post. He was very interested in women's liberation. His works include the *Arif-nama* and the *Hijab-nama*. He died in Tehran AH 1345/AD 1926.

JAHAN MALIK KHATUN, daughter of Jalal ud-Din Mas'ud Shah of the Inju ruling family in Fars, southern Iran, born second half of the eighth century AH/fourteenth century AD in Shiraz, where she was a contemporary of Hafiz.

JAHANBANI, Parvin, born AD 1965 in Ahvaz, Khuzistan, in southwestern Iran. She is married with three children. A graduate in business studies, she has recently started to write poetry, which she describes as 'words from my heart', and feels passionately about the issue of women and their lack of support in society.

JAMI, Maulana Nur al-Din 'Abdur-Rahman, born AH 817/AD 1414. His works include the *Haft Aurang* (Seven thrones) with 'Laili and Majnun' and other stories, 'Yusuf and Zulaikha' and 'Salaman and Absal'. He died AH 895/AD 1490.

KASRA AFSHAR, Laila, a woman poet born AD 1939–40, died 1989–90.

KATOUZIAN, Homa, born AD 1942. Social scientist, historian and literary critic, currently Iran Heritage Research Fellow at St Antony's College, Oxford, and a member of the Oriental Institute, University of Oxford. *Khisht-i Kham* (*A Song of Innocence*) was first published in Tehran SH 1377/AD 1998 and was reprinted five years later.

KHAJU KIRMANI, Kamal ud-Din Abu'ul 'Ata, born AH 679/AD 1280–81, died in Shiraz AH 753/AD 1352 or AH 762/AD 1361.

KHAYYAM, Ghiyas al-Din Abu'l-fath Umar bin Ibrahim, known as Umar Khayyam, born *c.* AH 412/AD 1021–2 in Nishabur, eastern Iran. He is said to have studied and developed a close friendship with Nizamu'l Mulk, the famous Seljuq minister of Sultan Malik Shah, and Hasan Sabbah of the Assassins. Trained as a scientist, he was an astronomer, mathematician, philosopher and physicist and successfully introduced calendar reforms in AD 1079. He died AH 515/AD 1122 in Nishabur. His *ruba'iyat* (quatrain) were first translated into English by Edward Fitzgerald in 1859.

MAHASTI GANJAVI, born in Khujand. Her name was Manizheh but her father nick-named her Mahasti (like a moon) because of her beauty. After his death she and her mother moved to Ganja (modern Republic of Azerbaijan). She later travelled to Zanjan in western Iran, Balkh (modern Afghanistan) and settled at the court of the Seljuq ruler Sultan Sanjar (AH 511–52/AD 1118–58) in Marv, where she is supposed to have met Umar Khayyam. She returned to Ganja and married. She died *c.* AH 613/AD 1217.

MAULANA JALAL AL-DIN BALKHI, known also as Maulavi and Rumi, born in Balkh (modern Afghanistan) AH 604/AD 1207. His family left Balkh for fear of the invading Mongols and via Damascus arrived in Konya in Turkey *c.* AH 618/AD 1221–2. He wrote the *Kulliyat-i Shams* (Complete poems of Shams) under the name of Shams-i Tabrizi. His Masnavi Ma'navi in six books is important for Sufi (mystic) philosophy and ethics. He died in Konya AH 671/AD 1273

MOSHIRI, Fereydoun, born AD 1925. From an early age he learned about classical Persian poetry from his father. He died in Tehran in 2000.

MU'IZZI NISHABURI, Amir ul Shu'ara Abu Abdallah Muhammad of Nishabur, born in Khurasan, eastern Iran. The son of a poet, he was attached to the court of the Seljuq ruler Sultan Malik Shah at Herat, Nishabur and Isfahan. He died c. AH 521/AD 1127.

NASIBI GILANI, born in Gilan, northern Iran. He moved to Tabriz as a young man, during the reign of Shah Isma'il (AH 907–30/AD 1501–24), and died there AH 944/AD 1537.

NIZAMI GANJAVI, Hakim Jamal al-Din Abu Muhammad Ilyas, born between AH 535 and 540/AD 1140–46 in Ganja (modern Republic of Azerbaijan). His epics include *Khusrau and Shirin*, *Laili and Majnun*, *Haft Paikar* (Seven Pictures) and *Iskandar-nama* (The Alexander Saga). Five of his epics were later put together in the *Khamsa* (Quintet).

RABA'A Qazdari Balkhi lived during the 4th century AH/10th century AD and was a contemporary of Rudaki. Her father Ka'b was supposedly of Arab origin and she was comfortable in both the Persian and Arabic languages. She fell in love with a slave and was killed by her own brother.

RUDAKI, Abu Abdallah Ja'far, born in Samarkand (modern Uzbekistan), was a blind bard of the Samanid court of Amir Nasr II (AH 301–31/AD 914–43) and his learned minister Abu'l Fazl Bal'ami. Died AH 329/AD 940–1.

RUMI: *see* Maulana Jalal al-Din Balkhi

SA'DI Shirazi, Muslah al-Din Abu Muhammad 'Abdallah, born c. AH 610–15/AD 1213–19 in Shiraz, southern Iran. He studied at the Nizamiya (university) of Baghdad and travelled widely, including Damascus. The *Bustan* (Orchard) was composed immediately after his return to Shiraz, followed a year later by the *Gulistan* (Rose garden). He died in Shiraz c. AH 691/AD 1291–2.

SARKHOSH, Mirza Yahya Khan, born AH 1277/AD 1860 in Tafrish, central Iran. After studying with his father and brother, he went to Khorramabad and then Khuzistan in southern Iran to pursue his studies. A competent calligrapher, he took up employment as a clerk. In AH 1308/AD 1890 he joined the British Legation in Tehran and was appointed First Clerk in 1903. He died in Tehran AH 1338/AD 1919.

SHAHRIYAR, Muhammad Hussein Bihjat Tabrizi, born Tabriz AD 1906. He began medical studies after secondary school education in Tehran, but did not complete his course. He died in 1988.

YOUSEFI, Nahid, a modern Iranian woman poet.

# FURTHER READING

Arberry, A. J. (ed.), *Fifty Poems of Hafiz* (Cambridge, 1962)

Arberry, A. J., *Shiraz: Persian City of Saints and Poets* (Norman, Oklahoma, 1960)

Atkinson, J. A., *The Loves of Laili and Majnun* (London, 1894)

Bowen, J. C. E., *Poems from the Persian*, 4th edn (Ipswich, Suffolk, 1985)

Browne, E. G., *Literary History of Persia*, vols I–IV (Cambridge, 1951)

Canby, S. R., *Persian Painting* (London, 1993)

Curtis, V. S., *Persian Myths* (London, 2000)

*Encyclopaedia of Islam* (Leiden, 1960–)

Fitzgerald, E., *Rubaiyat of Omar Khayyam* (New York)

Fitzgerald, E., *Salaman and Absal* (London, 1904)

Goethe, J. W., *West-östlicher Diwan* (1819)

Grabar, O. and Robinson, C. (eds), *Islamic Art and Literature* (Princeton, 2001)

Levy, R., *The Epic of the Kings* (London and Boston, 1977)

Nashat, G. and Beck, L. (eds.), *Women in Iran from the Rise of Islam to 1800* (Chicago, 2003)

Rypka, J., 'Poets and prose writers of the late Saljuq and Mongol periods', in Boyle, J. A. (ed.), *Cambridge History of Iran 5: The Saljuq and Mongol Periods* (Cambridge, 1968), pp. 550 ff

Rypka, J., *History of Iranian Literature* (Dordrecht, 1968)

Safa, Z., *Tarikh-i adabiyat dar Iran* (History of Literature in Iran), 5 vols (Tehran, AS 1332–78/AD 1953–99)

Simpson, M. S., *Sultan Ibrahim Mirza's* Haft Awrang: *A Princely Manuscript from Sixteenth-century Iran* (London and New Haven, 1997)

Tajbakhsh, G., *Zan, sha'r va andisha* (Woman, poetry and thought) (Tehran, AH 1378/AD 1999)

Thackston, W. M., 'The Diwan of Khata'i: Pictures for the Poetry of Shah Isma'il I', *Asian Art*, vol. 1, no. 4 (Fall 1988)

Warner, A. G. and E., *The Shahnama of Firdausi*, 10 vols (London, 1905–25)

Washington, P. (ed.), *Persian Poems*, Everyman's Library (London, 2000)

Yarshater, E. (ed.), *Encyclopedia Iranica* (New York, 1985–)

Yarshater, E., 'Persian Literature', in Holt, P. M, Lambton, A. K. S. and Lewis, B. (eds), *Cambridge History of Islam 2: The Further Islamic Lands: Islamic Society and Civilization II* (Cambridge, 1970), pp. 671 ff

# ILLUSTRATION REFERENCES

Photographs © The Trustees of the British Museum, Department of Asia (OA) or Department of the Ancient Near East (ANE), courtesy of the Department of Photography and Imaging, unless otherwise noted.

*page*

2    *see page 27*

6    Vesta Sarkhosh Curtis

15    OA 1969.6-16.03

17    OA 1920.9-17.0298(3)

19    OA 1948.12-11.023, Bequest of Sir Bernard Eckstein Bt

21    OA 1920.9-17.0295

23    Nasser D. Khalili Collection of Islamic Art, MSS 1030.8, folio 516b

25    OA 1922.7-11.02

27    OA 1948.10-9.057, P. C. Manuk and Miss G. M. Coles Collection, acquired through the National Art Collections Fund

29    OA 1921.6-14.01(5), Bequeathed by Baroness Zouche

31    ANE 1994.6-21.1

33    OA 2000.7-24.04, courtesy of the artist

35    OA 1983.3-15.01(25)

37    OA 1921.6-14.01(8), Bequeathed by Baroness Zouche

39    OA 1948.12-11.013, Bequest of Sir Bernard Eckstein Bt

41    OA 1920.9-17.0274

43    OA 1974.6-17.03(1)

45    OA 1934.10-13.02, Bequest of Sir Bernard Eckstein Bt

47    OA 1930.4-12.02

49    OA 1988.4-23.044

*page*

51    OA 1914.4-7.07

53    OA 1920.9-17.0275

55    OA 1920.9-17.0278(2)

57    OA 1988.4-23.034

59    OA 1974.6-17.03(84)

61    OA 1969.6-16.04

63    OA 1948.12-11.02, Bequest of Sir Bernard Eckstein Bt

65    OA 1948.12-11.015, Bequest of Sir Bernard Eckstein Bt

67    OA 1920.9-17.0258

69    OA 1920.9-17.0271

71    OA 1948.12-11.011, Bequest of Sir Bernard Eckstein Bt

73    OA 1920.9-17.0298(4)

75    OA 1930.6-7.015

77    OA 1948.12-11.020, Bequest of Sir Bernard Eckstein Bt

79    OA 1948.12-11.016, Bequest of Sir Bernard Eckstein Bt

81    OA 1974.6-17.015(23)

83    OA 1983.3-15.01(22)

85    OA 1983.3-15.01(24)

87    OA 1920.9-17.0301

89    OA 1921.6-14.01(2), Bequeathed by Baroness Zouche

91    OA 1948.12-11.08, Bequest of Sir Bernard Eckstein Bt